STORIES
of the
PROPHETS

YAYASAN PENDIDIKAN KHALIFAH (433502-X) is a non-profit organisation that focuses on spreading the Khalifah Method through education, mainly via two of its schools namely Khalifah Model School in Ampang and Khalifah Model Secondary School in Salak Tinggi, Selangor. They can be contacted at 427, Jalan 2, Taman Ampang Utama, 68000 Ampang, Selangor.

ABIDEEN BOOKS is an imprint under Abideen Publishing operating at Ostia Bangi Business Avenue in Bandar Baru Bangi, Selangor.

Copyright © Aqtar Mohamed Ummar

This book is in copyright. Subject to statutory exception and to the provisions of relevant collective licensing agreements, no reproduction of any part may take place without the written permission of Yayasan Pendidikan Khalifah

First published in October 2017
Publisher: Yayasan Pendidikan Khalifah & Abideen Publishing
Project Director: Hazwani binti Abdullah (Yayasan Pendidikan Khalifah)
Chief Editor: Ahmad Shakir bin Salleh (sharkpmc@gmail.com)
Author: Aqtar Mohamed Ummar
Typesetting & Illustration: Rasydan Fitri
Cover Design: Rasydan Fitri (rasydanfitri@gmail.com)

Cataloguing-in-Publication data:
STORIES of the PROPHETS / AQTAR MOHAMED UMMAR
ISBN 978-967-15422-0-0
1. Prophets in the Qur'an
2. Prophet, pre-Islamic. I. Title.
297.246

Printed by:
Firdaus Press Sdn. Bhd.
Books published by Yayasan Pendidikan Khalifah can be purchased with special discount for education and training purposes. Discounts for sales agents are also offered. For inquiry, please contact us at abideenbooks@gmail.com

STORIES
—— *of the* ——
PROPHETS

selected stories retold by
AQTAR MOHAMED UMMAR

*For my mother,
Gulnarabibi Noor Mohamed,
the illuminating sun of my days and
the guiding star of my nights.*

FOREWORD

All praise is due to Allah for giving me the ability and strength to complete this small book on selected stories of the prophets, focusing on the story of Sayyidina Musa (a.s.), the prophet most mentioned in the Quran. I chose these particular stories because they are the ones I am most familiar with and which I believe contain core moral values that need to be rekindled in our times.

I have used simple language in a conversational style, as if I was telling the stories to the readership in person, as I feel this would make it more interesting to read. The book is not an academic piece of writing which requires great focus and attention. It is for leisure reading and can be read by older children/teenagers and adults alike without much difficulty insya-Allah.

There is no novelty with regard to the knowledge contained within this book. Whatever I have written has already been discussed in exquisite detail in traditional works of tafseer by the great scholars of the past. I have only attempted to summarize a tiny portion of that knowledge - which I have gained by studying the Quran through lectures online and offline with various teachers as well

Foreword

as reading famous books of tafseer like Tafsir Ibn Kathir - which I hope will be beneficial to anyone who reads the book and I seek Allah's reward therefrom. Suggestions for improvements or corrections are welcome. I should mention, even if just in passing, that I am grateful to my sister, Alisia Nur Ummar for proofreading the book and giving comments for improvement. May Allah reward her abundantly.

Finally, as is the case with any work, this book cannot be perfect, for perfection belongs only to Allah and there is no protection from error save by Allah's leave. May Allah accept.

Aqtar Mohamed Ummar
7th October 2016
Khalifah Model School Secondary

CONTENTS

Sayyidina Musa (a.s.)
From Manslaughter to Messenger 1
The Damsels in Distress 6
Acknowledging the Abilities of Others 11
"And speak to him (Pharaoh) with gentle speech..." 16
Musa's Encounter with Khidr (peace be upon them both)
The Journey Begins 19
Mercy Before Knowledge 29
The Ship That Almost Sank 32
The Necessary Death Of A Child 40
The Righteous Father 46

Sayyidina Adam (a.s.) and Repentance 53

Sayyidina Nuh's (a.s.) Exhortation to Seek Forgiveness 62

Sayyidina Ibrahim (a.s.) and The Noble Guests 64

Sayyidina Ya'kub (a.s.) And The Tears of Sadness 68

Sayyidina Yusof (a.s.) and The Grand Design of Allah 74

Sayyidina Daawood and The Judgment of His Son (Peace be Upon Them Both) 80

Sayyidina Sulaiman (a.s.) and The Ants 85

FROM MANSLAUGHTER TO MESSENGER

Prophet Musa (a.s.) is one of the 5 Messengers of Strong Resolve (ulul 'azmi) and perhaps the greatest prophet of the Children of Israel. His story is the one that is most told in the Quran in different surahs (chapters). We learn in surah al-Qasas about an incident that would set him on an adventure which would lead to him becoming a Messenger of God.

This incident ironically however is not one anybody would be proud of. He had accidentally killed a Copt who was arguing with a person from amongst the Children of Israel. He struck him once without any intention to kill, but the man died anyway.

Musa (a.s.) of course was shocked himself and attributed the evil that had happened to Syaitan. He immediately repented to Allah, and Allah immediately forgave him, for Allah is indeed Most Forgiving, Most Merciful.

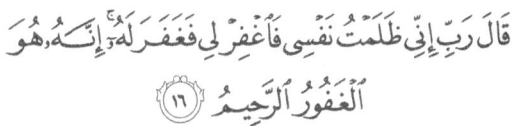

"He said: "My Lord! Verily, I have wronged myself,

so forgive me." Then He forgave him. Verily, He is Oft-Forgiving, the Most Merciful." (al-Qasas 28:16)

Allah loves those who turn to Him in repentance after committing a sin. In fact, He loves to forgive so much that a hadith tells us, if we were a people who never sinned, Allah would replace us with another people who would sin and then turn to Him in repentance so He could forgive them:

Prophet Muhammad (peace be upon him) said: "I swear by Him in whose hand is my soul, if you were a people who did not commit sin, Allah would take you away and replace you with a people who would sin and then seek Allah's forgiveness so He could forgive them." [Sahīh Muslim (2687)]

Going back to prophet Musa's (a.s.) unintentional crime, Allah not only forgave him but raised him to high rank of becoming one of the greatest Messengers of God. This teaches us that committing a sin, even if it is very grave will not result in our inevitable doom if we turn to Allah in repentance and strive to make things right.

Musa (a.s.) swore to Allah to never help any criminal after that incident:

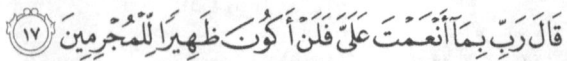

He said: "My Lord! For that with which You have favoured me, I will never more be a helper of the Mujrimûn (criminals)!" (al-Qasas 28:17)

People may have had bad beginnings but Allah can erase that painful past and bring forth something so great we could not even imagine. We will surely meet many people like this in our lives, people whose pasts were tainted with the darkness of sin, but they have turned over a new leaf. What we must never ever do then, is bring up the past of someone who has repented and is trying to start things over.

People usually resort to this dirty trick when they are not happy with someone due to an argument or disagreement. This abominable act of bringing up someone's past shifts the focus away from one's self, as was done by none other than Pharaoh, the most abominable of all human beings to have ever lived, when Musa (a.s.) came to him with the Message and to deliver the children of Israel.

His words are preserved in surah Asy-Syu'ara as a lesson for us:

وَلَهُمْ عَلَىَّ ذَنۢبٌ فَأَخَافُ أَن يَقۡتُلُونِ ۝ قَالَ كَلَّا ۖ فَٱذۡهَبَا بِـَٔايَٰتِنَآ ۖ إِنَّا مَعَكُم مُّسۡتَمِعُونَ ۝ فَأۡتِيَا فِرۡعَوۡنَ فَقُولَآ إِنَّا رَسُولُ رَبِّ ٱلۡعَٰلَمِينَ ۝ أَنۡ أَرۡسِلۡ مَعَنَا بَنِىٓ إِسۡرَٰٓءِيلَ ۝ قَالَ أَلَمۡ نُرَبِّكَ فِينَا وَلِيدًا وَلَبِثۡتَ فِينَا مِنۡ عُمُرِكَ سِنِينَ ۝

وَفَعَلْتَ فَعْلَتَكَ ٱلَّتِي فَعَلْتَ وَأَنتَ مِنَ ٱلْكَٰفِرِينَ ﴿١٩﴾

"And they have upon me a [claim due to] sin, so I fear that they will kill me. [Allāh] said, "No. Go both of you with Our signs; indeed, We are with you, listening. Go to Pharaoh and say, 'We are the messengers of the Lord of the worlds, [Commanded to say], "Send with us the Children of Israel."' "[Pharaoh] said, "Did we not raise you among us as a child, and you remained among us for years of your life? And [then] you did your deed which you did, and you were of the ungrateful."" (Asy-Syua'ara 26:14-19)

Thus, if we bring up someone's hurtful past just because we're angry, displeased with him or her, then we have become pharaohs ourselves, wal'iyazubillah, we seek Allah's refuge from walking in the footsteps of those who are doomed to the Fire.

And as for those of us who have done bad things in the past, remember that all hope is not lost. The doors of mercy are always open. Let us turn to Allah in sincere repentance, seek His forgiveness, turn over a new leaf and constantly make dua' for guidance as Musa (a.s.) did. He was constantly making dua' to Allah to guide him, to save him from those who are evil, to make his affairs easy for him etc.

Musa A.S: From Manslaughter to Messenger

We will be surprised at how Allah will bless us. Indeed, in Musa's (a.s.) case, it was from the crime of manslaughter, to becoming one of the greatest Messengers of God to walk upon the earth, Subhanallah! What a blessing!

DAMSELS IN DISTRESS

Surah al-Qasas contains the bulk of Musa's (a.s.) life before he became a prophet. Previously, we saw how he mistakenly killed a Copt but then repented. After that incident, he fled the city because his crime was discovered and the authorities wanted to kill him. He fled towards Madyan whilst seeking the guidance of Allah:

وَجَآءَ رَجُلٌ مِّنْ أَقْصَا ٱلْمَدِينَةِ يَسْعَىٰ قَالَ يَٰمُوسَىٰٓ إِنَّ ٱلْمَلَأَ يَأْتَمِرُونَ بِكَ لِيَقْتُلُوكَ فَٱخْرُجْ إِنِّى لَكَ مِنَ ٱلنَّٰصِحِينَ ﴿٢٠﴾ فَخَرَجَ مِنْهَا خَآئِفًا يَتَرَقَّبُ قَالَ رَبِّ نَجِّنِى مِنَ ٱلْقَوْمِ ٱلظَّٰلِمِينَ ﴿٢١﴾ وَلَمَّا تَوَجَّهَ تِلْقَآءَ مَدْيَنَ قَالَ عَسَىٰ رَبِّىٓ أَن يَهْدِيَنِى سَوَآءَ ٱلسَّبِيلِ ﴿٢٢﴾

And a man came from the farthest end of the city, running. He said, "O Musa, indeed the eminent ones are conferring over you [intending] to kill you, so leave [the city]; indeed, I am to you of the sincere advisors." So he left it, fearful and anticipating [apprehension]. He said, "My Lord, save me from the wrongdoing people." And when he directed himself toward Madyan, he said, "Perhaps my

Lord will guide me to the sound way." (Al-Qasas 28: 20-22)

Upon reaching a watering place, he saw two damsels waiting to water their flock:

$$وَلَمَّا وَرَدَ مَاءَ مَدْيَنَ وَجَدَ عَلَيْهِ أُمَّةً مِنَ النَّاسِ يَسْقُونَ وَوَجَدَ مِن دُونِهِمُ ٱمْرَأَتَيْنِ تَذُودَانِ قَالَ مَا خَطْبُكُمَا قَالَتَا لَا نَسْقِي حَتَّىٰ يُصْدِرَ ٱلرِّعَاءُ وَأَبُونَا شَيْخٌ كَبِيرٌ ۝ فَسَقَىٰ لَهُمَا ثُمَّ تَوَلَّىٰٓ إِلَى ٱلظِّلِّ فَقَالَ رَبِّ إِنِّي لِمَا أَنزَلْتَ إِلَيَّ مِنْ خَيْرٍ فَقِيرٌ ۝$$

And when he came to the water [i.e., well] of Madyan, he found there a crowd of people watering [their flocks], and he found aside from them two women driving back [their flocks]. He said, "What is your circumstance?" They said, "We do not water until the shepherds dispatch [their flocks]; and our father is an old man." So he watered [their flocks] for them; then he went back to the shade and said, "My Lord, indeed I am, for whatever good You would send down to me, in need." (Al-Qasas 28: 23-24)

First, notice how throughout this ordeal, Musa (a.s.) is completely conscious of Allah, asking Him to save, guide and help him. One can almost hear the desperation

in his voice in the last dua', where he beseeches Allah, stating his dire need for any good that Allah will send down upon him.

The dependence of the prophets on God and their continuous beseeching Him gives them the strength to undergo immense trials. In the same way, if Allah is constantly on our minds, we too will be able to face trials under which ordinary folk would break. God consciousness and constant remembrance of Him can make us extraordinary.

Now let us look at Musa's (a.s.) response to the situation at the watering area. One can only imagine how tired he must have been after travelling so far from Egypt to Madyan, yet he was cognizant of what was going on around him. He saw two young girls who seemed out of place, and so he approached them to ask them what was their problem.

This is such a fascinating response. A really tired man after a long journey, who himself probably needs water to quench his thirst, decides instead to help two damsels before sitting down to rest under the shade of a tree. There are so many lessons to derive from this story. The righteous and God conscious are always aware of the needs of those around them, even if they are strangers or members of the society who are usually deemed to be underserving of respect, like women. Not only that, they go out of their way even if they are in a state of desperation themselves, to do whatever they can to help others.

This story is particularly important for those among us who go to extremes in our strictness with regard to mingling with the opposite sex.

Musa (a.s.) did not say to himself, "Oh my god! two women out in the desert alone! How shameless!" or "Ya Allah, these two women look like they need help, but I can't help them because they are a source of fitnah! I must lower my gaze and pretend they don't exist lest my iman gets jeopardized!" No, he said none of those things. He approached them, asked them what the problem was, helped them, and went to rest without any further unnecessary chat.

His response to the situation is the perfect balance between unnecessary and shameless mingling on the one hand and extreme gender segregation on the other.

May Allah guide us to be an ummah of the middle path, 'ummatan wasatan', as exemplified by the action of Musa (a.s.) in this incident, so we may be an example for humanity. Ameen.

ACKNOWLEDGING THE ABILITIES OF OTHERS

One of the reasons I love the story of Musa (a.s.) in the Quran is because the hero i.e. Musa (a.s.) is not the perfect and charismatic knight in shining armour one expects.

He had a bad past as we saw in the previous chapter 'From Manslaughter to Messenger', and he also had a stutter. Let us imagine ourselves for a second being asked to speak on a stage in front of a group of strange people. We would get a dry mouth, we would forget what to say, we would get butterflies in our stomach and we would surely stutter a little even if we were used to giving public speeches.

The situation gets worse if we are asked to speak in front of people more powerful than ourselves. Now imagine Musa's (a.s.) situation. Allah asked him to go and deliver the Message to Pharaoh, who is probably the most tyrannical ruler who ever lived, and ask him to let the Children of Israel go.

It is bad enough that Musa had a stutter even in ordinary speech. Now he had to speak in front of Pharaoh in his court filled with his malevolent chiefs, with the knowledge that they want to kill him for the crime he committed years ago.

And he is supposed to challenge Pharaoh's belief that there is a God mightier than him! Even the most eloquent person would be speechless if they had to face Pharaoh in such a circumstance to deliver such a message. That is why Musa (a.s.) made the very famous dua' we all know when he received this command from Allah:

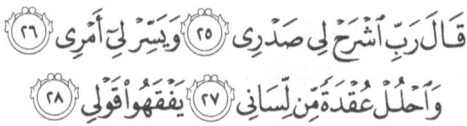

[Musa] said, "My Lord, expand [i.e., relax] for me my breast [with assurance]

And ease for me my task

And untie the knot from my tongue

That they may understand my speech. (Taha 20:25-28)

And he also made the following dua' which can be found in surah Al-Qasas:

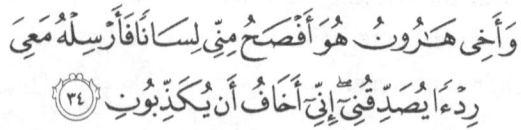

"And my brother Harun is more fluent than me in tongue, so send him with me as support, verifying me. Indeed, I fear that they will deny me." (Al-Qasas 28:34)

Musa A.S: Acknowledging the Ability of Others

My focus here is on the second dua', of how he asked Allah jalla wa 'ala to strengthen him with his brother Harun (a.s.) because the latter was more fluent than him in speech. Such is the humility of the prophets, which makes them realize their shortcomings whilst acknowledging and benefiting from the capabilities of others, even if those 'others' are of a lower status (Musa was the main prophet of the Children of Israel, whilst Harun, also a prophet, was of a lower rank).

We all have our own strengths which we can use to benefit others, and weaknesses which we must realize so as to remain humble. Allah created us to complement one another. Nobody is able to do everything, because nobody is perfect, for perfection belongs to Allah alone.

Contrast this with the attitude of Iblis when he was commanded to prostrate before Adam (a.s.):

$$\text{قَالَ أَنَا۠ خَيْرٌ مِّنْهُ ۖ خَلَقْتَنِي مِن نَّارٍ وَخَلَقْتَهُۥ مِن طِينٍ ﴿٧٦﴾}$$

He said, "I am better than him. You created me from fire and created him from clay." (Sad 38: 76)

Thus is the attitude of Iblis and his followers: the racists, the Nazis, the social Darwinists, who think themselves to be superior to others, whose arrogance is cursed by Allah and all of creation.

Abdullah ibn Mas'ud reported: The Prophet, peace and blessings be upon him, said, "No one who has the weight of a seed of arrogance in his heart will enter Paradise." Someone said, "But a man loves to have beautiful clothes and shoes." The Prophet said, "Verily, Allah is beautiful and He loves beauty. Arrogance means rejecting the truth and looking down on people." [Muslim]

I included the second part of the hadith so we do not get the wrong idea about arrogance. Wearing beautiful clothes in itself is okay and in fact encouraged, unless it is accompanied with a feeling of pride to show off.

May Allah adorn us with the virtue of humility, so we may see the good in others and the weakness in ourselves, and may He protect us from the evil of arrogance, which destroys any good we have done, as it destroyed Iblis, who was disgraced, relegated to a cursed life despite initially being among the ranks of the righteous angels. Ameen.

"AND SPEAK TO HIM (PHARAOH) WITH GENTLE SPEECH..."

In chapter 20 of the Quran (surah Taha), Allah narrates to us the story of Musa (a.s.). Upon receiving Messengership, Allah commands Musa (a.s.) to go to Pharaoh:

$$\text{اذْهَبْ أَنتَ وَأَخُوكَ بِآيَاتِي وَلَا تَنِيَا فِي ذِكْرِي ﴿٤٢﴾ اذْهَبَا إِلَىٰ فِرْعَوْنَ إِنَّهُ طَغَىٰ ﴿٤٣﴾ فَقُولَا لَهُ قَوْلًا لَّيِّنًا لَّعَلَّهُ يَتَذَكَّرُ أَوْ يَخْشَىٰ ﴿٤٤﴾}$$

"Go, you and your brother, with My signs and do not slacken in My remembrance. Go, both of you, to Pharaoh. Indeed, he has transgressed. And speak to him with gentle speech that perhaps he may be reminded or fear [Allāh]." (Taha 20: 42-44)

The Pharaoh ruling over Egypt at the time (his name is not mentioned in the Quran like many other characters, for what is important is not who these people were but what we can learn from them) was a tyrant who enslaved the children of Israel. Not only did he mistreat them severely, he also killed their sons and let their daughters live.

Musa A.S: "And Speak to Him with Gentle Speech..."

To cut a long story short, Musa (a.s.) was chosen by Allah to be the Messenger to deliver the Children of Israel from the tyranny of Pharaoh. Despite all the evils committed by the tyrant, Allah commanded Musa (a.s.) to go to him and speak gently first, for perhaps he might be admonished and change his ways.

Of course Allah in His infinite knowledge and wisdom knew that the Pharaoh was not going to change one bit, but He wanted to teach Musa (a.s.) and by extension all of us that we should never write people off straight away however bad they may appear to us. This is key when doing da'wah. We should always approach people with an open mind and do not let their evils cause us to be judgmental from the word go.

If Allah had commanded Musa (a.s.) to speak gently to Pharaoh, one of the most evil and arrogant of people to ever walk upon this earth, just in case he may benefit from the advice despite Allah knowing full well those gentle words were not going to change a thing, what then is our excuse for not being gentle when approaching people far less in evilness, not knowing at all whether our advice may benefit them or not?

Judging people to be hopeless especially before even trying to advise them is arrogant. Judgment belongs to Allah and Allah alone and it may be that Allah will forgive that person whom we deemed hopeless, and instead throw us into the Fire for our arrogance.

So let us advise and remind others gently and never consider anyone to be beyond hope because we don't know that and acting like we do will only earn us Allah's wrath, the inevitable consequence of which is entry into the Fire of Jahannam. Wal'iyazubillah.

MUSA'S ENCOUNTER WITH KHIDR (PEACE BE UPON THEM BOTH): *THE JOURNEY BEGINS*

As we all know, the Prophet (p.b.u.h.) told us to read surah al-Kahf every Friday: *"Whoever reads Soorat al-Kahf on the day of Jumu'ah, will have a light that will shine from him from one Friday to the next."* (Narrated by al-Haakim, 2/399; al-Bayhaqi, 3/249. It was classed as saheeh by Shaykh al-Albaani in Saheeh al-Jaami', 6470)

In this surah, there are four main stories about four different kinds of trials we face in our lives. The first is the trial of faith in the story of the seven sleepers in the cave, and then there's the trial of wealth in the story of the two friends, the third is the trial of knowledge in the story of Musa and Khidr (a.s.) and the last one is the trial of power in the story of Dhul Qarnayn.

For now, let us focus on the third story in the surah, the story about the trial of knowledge.

The story begins:

وَإِذْ قَالَ مُوسَىٰ لِفَتَىٰهُ لَآ أَبْرَحُ حَتَّىٰٓ أَبْلُغَ مَجْمَعَ ٱلْبَحْرَيْنِ أَوْ أَمْضِىَ حُقُبًا ﴿٦٠﴾

"And [mention] when Musa said to his servant, "I will not cease [traveling] until I reach the junction of the two seas or continue for a long period."" (Al-Kahf 18:60)

To understand this story, we need a little background information which we can obtain from the hadiths of Prophet (p.b.u.h.) on the matter. The whole hadith can be found in Sahih Bukhari [Book 3 Hadith 124], but I will try to summarize the main points.

One day Musa (a.s.) was questioned by his people, the Children of Israel, as to who was the most knowledgeable person on earth. Naturally, Musa (a.s.) said he was, since he was the prophet of the time.

Allah however was not happy with this answer of Musa (a.s.) for he had not referred the knowledge to Allah, and so Allah commanded him to look for a servant from among His servants, who had some knowledge which he did not possess and this person could be found at the meeting of the two seas. (There is no need to get bogged down with the details of where these two seas were. Allah did not feel it important for us to know, and so we should just leave it be.)

Thus the story begins with the words of Musa (a.s.) as per the verse above. Perhaps the first lesson we can learn from this is Musa's (a.s.) enthusiasm to seek knowledge. Remember, he was THE prophet of his time, even greater than Khidr (a.s.) He had no need of Khidr's (a.s.) knowledge because he had far more knowledge than Khidr (a.s.) If we had been in his shoes, perhaps we might have just told Allah (Musa (a.s.) is known as kaleemullah since he had the privilege of speaking to Allah directly without the agency of Archangel Jibril), " O Allah, chill man. What's the big deal? I'm going to Jannah anyway. Why the need for all the unnecessary hardwork??"

But no, Musa (a.s.) would travel far just to gain some extra knowledge from this other slave of Allah called Khidr (a.s.) (peace be upon them both). He would not miss out on an opportunity to better his current level of knowledge despite him being guaranteed Jannah.

What then is our excuse for being so lazy when it comes to seeking knowledge, especially since most of us sadly, are hardly Jannah material? Do we expect Allah to pop a book down from the heavens onto our laps while we're watching the latest sitcom or soap opera so we can browse through that Divine book while watching the show?

Knowledge requires hard work and persistence. Knowledge is the first step towards improving ourselves and our relationship with Allah, for it is only with knowledge will we be able to distinguish right from wrong, deeds which Allah loves from those He despises even if they may seem right and etc. Was not the first word to be revealed 'iqra' which means read? We should be an ummah of knowledge, for knowledge is power and it is with knowledge that Allah will raise our ranks.

$$يَٰٓأَيُّهَا ٱلَّذِينَ ءَامَنُوٓا۟ إِذَا قِيلَ لَكُمْ تَفَسَّحُوا۟ فِى ٱلْمَجَٰلِسِ فَٱفْسَحُوا۟ يَفْسَحِ ٱللَّهُ لَكُمْ ۖ وَإِذَا قِيلَ ٱنشُزُوا۟ فَٱنشُزُوا۟ يَرْفَعِ ٱللَّهُ ٱلَّذِينَ ءَامَنُوا۟ مِنكُمْ وَٱلَّذِينَ أُوتُوا۟ ٱلْعِلْمَ دَرَجَٰتٍ ۚ وَٱللَّهُ بِمَا تَعْمَلُونَ خَبِيرٌ ۝$$

"....And when you are told, "Arise," then arise; Allah will raise those who have believed among you and those who were given knowledge, by degrees. And Allah is Acquainted with what you do." (Al-Mujadilah 58:11)

May Allah make us of those who read; of those who strive to seek knowledge that is beneficial, to better ourselves and hence the ummah; and ultimately to gain His pleasure.

Let us continue with the story.

$$فَلَمَّا بَلَغَا مَجْمَعَ بَيْنِهِمَا نَسِيَا حُوتَهُمَا فَٱتَّخَذَ سَبِيلَهُۥ فِى ٱلْبَحْرِ سَرَبًا ۝ فَلَمَّا جَاوَزَا قَالَ لِفَتَىٰهُ ءَاتِنَا غَدَآءَنَا لَقَدْ لَقِينَا مِن سَفَرِنَا هَٰذَا نَصَبًا ۝ قَالَ أَرَءَيْتَ إِذْ أَوَيْنَآ إِلَى ٱلصَّخْرَةِ فَإِنِّى نَسِيتُ ٱلْحُوتَ وَمَآ أَنسَىٰنِيهُ إِلَّا ٱلشَّيْطَٰنُ أَنْ أَذْكُرَهُۥ ۚ وَٱتَّخَذَ سَبِيلَهُۥ فِى ٱلْبَحْرِ عَجَبًا ۝ قَالَ ذَٰلِكَ مَا$$

Musa A.S: The Journey Begins

$$كُنَّا نَبْغِ ۚ فَارْتَدَّا عَلَىٰ آثَارِهِمَا قَصَصًا ۝٦٤$$

"But when they reached the junction between them, they forgot their fish, and it took its course into the sea, slipping away. So when they had passed beyond it, [Musa] said to his boy, "Bring us our morning meal. We have certainly suffered in this, our journey, [much] fatigue."

He said, "Did you see when we retired to the rock? Indeed, I forgot [there] the fish. And none made me forget it except Iblis - that I should mention it. And it took its course into the sea amazingly".

[Musa] said, "That is what we were seeking." So they returned, following their footprints." (Al-Kahf 18: 61-64)

Allah told Musa (a.s.) the servant (Khidr (a.s.)) who was more learned than him could be found at the meeting of the two seas, and that he should take a dead fish kept in a vessel along with him on the journey. The point where the fish comes back to life and jumps into the sea in a miraculous way is where they will find Khidr (a.s.).

The journey was long, and as could be expected, Musa (a.s.) and his servant boy Yusha' ibn Nun, perhaps stopped a couple of times to rest. At one of those rest stops, Yusha' saw the fish coming back to life and jumping into the sea. Musa (a.s.) a.s. was asleep at the time and Yusha' did not want to wake him but unfortunately when

Musa (a.s.) woke up, Yusha' forgot to inform him of the miraculous sign, and so they both continued on their journey. They stopped to rest again sometime later and Musa (a.s.) told Yusha' to bring out the food they had prepared for the journey so they can have something to eat before moving on. While Yusha' was taking the food out from his bag, he suddenly remembered that the fish had escaped miraculously way back during the earlier stop. So he tells Musa (a.s.) about this and attributes his forgetfulness to Syaitan. Musa (a.s.) said, that was the point at which Khidr (a.s.) was supposed to be found and so they retraced their steps.

There are a couple of lessons we can take from the story thus far. First is that they prepared food for their journey because tawakkul requires effort on our part first. Musa (a.s.) did not just set out on his journey hoping for sustenance to come from the heavens. He got his boy-servant to prepare some food so they could eat and rejuvenate their strength along the way.

The seerah of our prophet (p.b.u.h.) is full of examples where he did all he could in his capacity as a human being before placing his trust in Allah, in all of his affairs. The true believer doesn't just 'place his trust in Allah without doing anything. That is laziness, not tawakkul. The true believer does all he can first, and then places his trust in Allah. Remember Maryam the mother of 'Isa a.s when she was in labour?

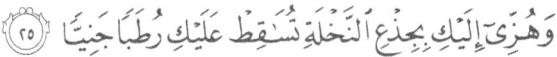

"And shake toward you the trunk of the palm tree; it will drop upon you ripe, fresh dates." (Maryam 19:25)

Subhanallah! She was in labour, and yet Allah told her to shake the trunk of the date palm tree so the dates would fall down. Shake the date palm tree! Can you imagine telling that to a woman when she is in labour? A response in the form of a slap across the face would be likely.

Of course Allah knew she was in no state to shake the trunk of a date palm tree, which is not some small soft stemmed plant! But Allah just wanted to teach her that NOTHING comes for free. Her effort would not have caused the fruits to fall. It was Allah who made the dates fall, but she had to put in some effort first.

Even when making decisions, one has to first do whatever one can to make an informed decision like consulting others, and then only place one's trust in Allah. Not wait for an angel dressed in white to come down and deliver the answer in a scroll on a platter of gold!

The next lesson is about how forgetfulness is attributed to Syaitan. This happens twice in the Quran, and the lesson is that we should always seek refuge in Allah from Syaitan if we are of those who frequently forget things, provided one does not have Alzheimer's or other types of dementias of course.

Another lesson from this part of the story is Musa's (a.s.) composure upon hearing what Yusha' said. Now imagine for a second if we were in a similar situation. We have walked so far so as to require another round of rest when our travelling companion says the point we were looking for was at the previous stop we made. We would probably lose our heads and do or say something to that companion for being so negligent and forgetful!

But look at how calm Musa (a.s.) was. Not a single word of rebuke. He just said that was the place they were looking for and so they both began to retrace their steps. There was no point whatsoever in blowing up in anger because that wouldn't have changed anything. The mistake was genuine, and anger was not going to solve anything.

In fact, it would've made the remainder of the journey very difficult because Yusha' would've felt bad for being scolded and Musa (a.s.) would've felt awkward to communicate with him further. Such scenarios often happen in our lives, especially with children. They make mistakes, but there is no point in rebuking them when the mistake was genuine.

Instead pardon and forgiveness is always better but certainly more difficult to practice. Thus Allah says to Prophet Muhammad regarding his response to the believers who disobeyed him during the battle of Uhud:

Musa A.S: The Journey Begins

فَبِمَا رَحْمَةٍ مِّنَ ٱللَّهِ لِنتَ لَهُمْ ۖ وَلَوْ كُنتَ فَظًّا غَلِيظَ ٱلْقَلْبِ لَٱنفَضُّوا۟ مِنْ حَوْلِكَ ۖ فَٱعْفُ عَنْهُمْ وَٱسْتَغْفِرْ لَهُمْ وَشَاوِرْهُمْ فِى ٱلْأَمْرِ ۖ فَإِذَا عَزَمْتَ فَتَوَكَّلْ عَلَى ٱللَّهِ ۚ إِنَّ ٱللَّهَ يُحِبُّ ٱلْمُتَوَكِّلِينَ ﴿١٠٩﴾

"It is a mercy from Allah that you were gentle with them. If you had been rough or hard of heart, they would have scattered from around you. So pardon them and ask forgiveness for them, and consult with them about the matter. Then when you have reached a firm decision, put your trust in Allah. Allah loves those who put their trust in Him." (Ali 'Imran 2:159)

MUSA'S ENCOUNTER WITH KHIDR (PEACE BE UPON THEM BOTH): *MERCY BEFORE KNOWLEDGE*

Let us continue with Musa's (a.s.) journey. He and his boy-servant Yusha' ibn Nun retraced their steps until they found Khidr (a.s.) where Allah told them he would be found, at the meeting of the two seas.

$$\text{فَوَجَدَا عَبۡدٗا مِّنۡ عِبَادِنَآ ءَاتَيۡنَٰهُ رَحۡمَةٗ مِّنۡ عِندِنَا وَعَلَّمۡنَٰهُ مِن لَّدُنَّا عِلۡمٗا ۝ قَالَ لَهُۥ مُوسَىٰ هَلۡ أَتَّبِعُكَ عَلَىٰٓ أَن تُعَلِّمَنِ مِمَّا عُلِّمۡتَ رُشۡدٗا ۝}$$

"And they found a servant from among Our servants to whom we had given mercy from us and had taught him from Us a [certain] knowledge. Musa (a.s.) said to him, "May I follow you on [the condition] that you teach me from what you have been taught of sound judgement?"" (Al-Kahf 18: 65-66)

This 'servant' that Allah speaks about is of course none other than Prophet Khidr (a.s.). He was called Khidr (a.s.) (Khadr in Arabic means green) because when he sat on a barren land, that area around him would turn green with vegetation as the Prophet (p.b.u.h) explained in various hadiths.

When Allah introduces Khidr (a.s.), He says, *"And they found a servant from among Our servants to whom we had given mercy from us and had taught him from Us a [certain] knowledge."*

Since the Quran is the Word of Allah, all things about it must be studied and taken into consideration, even the order of the words, for Allah the Most Wise places everything in its proper place.

In this verse, He mentions that this servant whom Musa (a.s.) is to meet, has been given mercy and has been taught knowledge. The order of blessings bestowed upon Khidr (a.s.) is Mercy first, then Knowledge.

And so the main lesson here for us is that, if we wish to benefit ourselves and those around us with our knowledge, we first must adorn our hearts with mercy, for if there is no mercy, then that knowledge will be of no use.

How often have we met fellow Muslims who are so stern and aggressive when it comes to giving advice, a listener would think we've committed a grave crime like murder requiring severe rebuking and a great outcry! It may have been a small issue like little kids making some noise in the mosque, but the response would be "IT IS

HARAAAAAAAAAAMMMMM TO BRING KIDS TO THE MOSQUE BECAUSE THEY MAKE SO MUCH NOISE!!!" Subhanallah!

Whoever to whom this 'advise' is directed will flee for their lives, lest they perish in the fiery breath of these overzealous, merciless people! So let us adorn our hearts with mercy and kindness, so others may benefit from our knowledge with ease, insya-Allah.

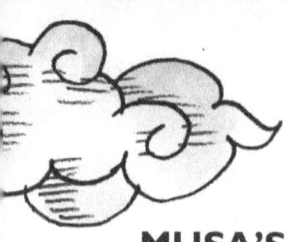

MUSA'S ENCOUNTER WITH KHIDR (PEACE BE UPON THEM BOTH): *THE SHIP THAT ALMOST SANK*

قَالَ لَهُۥ مُوسَىٰ هَلۡ أَتَّبِعُكَ عَلَىٰٓ أَن تُعَلِّمَنِ مِمَّا عُلِّمۡتَ رُشۡدٗا ۝ قَالَ إِنَّكَ لَن تَسۡتَطِيعَ مَعِيَ صَبۡرٗا ۝ وَكَيۡفَ تَصۡبِرُ عَلَىٰ مَا لَمۡ تُحِطۡ بِهِۦ خُبۡرٗا ۝ قَالَ سَتَجِدُنِيٓ إِن شَآءَ ٱللَّهُ صَابِرٗا وَلَآ أَعۡصِي لَكَ أَمۡرٗا ۝ قَالَ فَإِنِ ٱتَّبَعۡتَنِي فَلَا تَسۡـَٔلۡنِي عَن شَيۡءٍ حَتَّىٰٓ أُحۡدِثَ لَكَ مِنۡهُ ذِكۡرٗا ۝ فَٱنطَلَقَا حَتَّىٰٓ إِذَا رَكِبَا فِي ٱلسَّفِينَةِ خَرَقَهَاۖ قَالَ أَخَرَقۡتَهَا لِتُغۡرِقَ أَهۡلَهَا لَقَدۡ جِئۡتَ شَيۡـًٔا إِمۡرٗا ۝

Musa (a.s.) said to him, "May I follow you on that you teach me from what you have been taught of sound judgement?" He said, "Indeed, with me you will never be able to have patience.

And how can you have patience for what you do not encompass in knowledge?" [Musa] said, "You will find me, if Allah wills, patient, and I will not disobey you in [any] order."

He said, "Then if you follow me, do not ask me about anything until I myself mention of it to you."

Musa A.S: The Ship that Almost Sank

So they set out, until when they had embarked on the ship, al-Khidr (a.s.) tore it open. [Musa] said, "Have you torn it open to drown its people? You have certainly done a grave thing." (al-Kahf 18: 66-71)

The first few verses above demonstrate to us the manners required from a student of knowledge when seeking knowledge from a teacher. Musa (a.s.) did not demand, but instead asked for permission to follow Khidr (a.s.) in his travels so he may learn something of the knowledge that Khidr (a.s.) possessed. And we also learn here that the best way to acquire knowledge is to be in the company of one's teacher, which has been the main mode of transmission of knowledge in Islamic scholarship since the time of the Prophet (p.b.u.h).

Unfortunately, in this era of 'Shaykh Google', many of us, have beguiled ourselves into thinking that we can possess great knowledge without a teacher to lead and guide us, from whom we can learn not just new things but adaab as well. We must appreciate the fact that the best and most effective way to gain knowledge is to be with a teacher who not only imparts what he knows, but also teaches us how to use that knowledge wisely, either directly through instruction, or by our own observation.

Khidr (a.s.) tells Musa (a.s.) that he will not be able to bear with the things that he will do on his journey, for he does not possess the knowledge of the unseen that

Khidr (a.s.) has. Musa (a.s.) however insists and says he will be patient, Insya Allah i.e. If Allah Wills (One of this surah's main lessons is the importance of saying insya Allah which deserves a whole separate post). Khidr (a.s.) gives in but places a condition upon Musa (a.s.) that is he shall not ask anything about the events that will transpire, until Khidr (a.s.) himself elucidates the matter.

So the first of the three incidents is the story of the ship. Musa (a.s.) and Khidr (a.s.) were offered a boat ride by some fisherman who knew Khidr (a.s.) This is not mentioned in the verses, but in a long hadith in Sahih Bukhari. Upon embarking the ship, while the fishermen were busy perhaps, Khidr (a.s.) damaged the boat by creating a small hole that would cause the boat to sink slowly. The fishermen would have no choice but to turn back in order to save themselves.

Musa (a.s.) seeing this very unjust act blows up and asks Khidr (a.s.) in an angry tone as to why he would do such a terrible thing? Did Khidr (a.s.) want to drown the people of this boat?

Notice in the verse quoted above, Musa (a.s.) does not say "Have you torn it down to drown us?" Instead he says "Have you torn in down to drown its people?" Such are the hearts of the prophets. They always think about the wellbeing of others before their own. And if we wish to be successful callers to Islam, then we must adorn ourselves with this virtue of placing the needs of others before our own.

Khidr (a.s.) reminds Musa (a.s.) of his promise of being patient, not asking any questions. Musa (a.s.) quickly regains control of his emotions and realizes his mistake and apologizes.

Here we learn an important lesson that is to humbly admit one's mistakes and apologize. If we were onlookers to this situation, and certainly if we were in Musa's (a.s.) position, we would feel it justified to react in such a way, and that an apology is not warranted because Khidr (a.s.) had committed a great evil and should be scolded.

How can our judgment of the situation be wrong, right? But we have to realize, that often there is more than meets the eye, and so it is best not to jump to conclusions so very quickly before looking at the bigger picture of things, or at least inquiring about why such an act was carried out.

Now let us fast forward to a few verses ahead where Khidr (a.s.) explains why he damaged the boat.

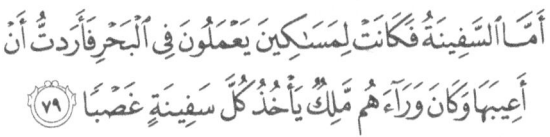

"As for the ship, it belonged to poor people working at sea. So I intended to cause defect in it as there

was after them a king who seized every [good] ship by force." (Al-Kahf 18:79)

See, there is indeed an explanation for what Khidr (a.s.) did! He damaged the ship because Allah had informed him of a king who would seize the property of these poor fishermen by force. By causing a defect to the ship, Khidr (a.s.) had saved the means of livelihood of the fishermen, as the king would not take anything that would be of no benefit to him. The fishermen on the other hand could repair it and then use it again later for fishing, rather than have the whole ship taken away.

So the lesson here and also in the other two incidents in the chronicles of Musa (a.s.) and Khidr (a.s.) which we will discuss in due course insya Allah, is that there is wisdom behind everything that happens to us. We may feel frustrated and angry when something bad happens to us, but Allah has used that incident to prevent a greater harm to us, which we may not be able to perceive now, but maybe later in future. The key is to be patient and place our trust in Allah, the Best Disposer of Affairs.

The other main lesson of this incident is the preservation of wealth that is used for the sake of Allah. Owing to the fact that these fishermen were generous with their ship, Allah preserved it for them. And so it is for us. When we spend our wealth in charity, Allah will preserve that wealth even if to our eyes it may seem like a loss.

This is especially difficult in the case of money, because how can money leaving our pockets be preserved?? It's gone! Gone now, but will be replaced with much more insya-Allah.

The key again is to be sincere and place our trust in Allah, the Best of Providers.

MUSA'S ENCOUNTER WITH KHIDR (PEACE BE UPON THEM BOTH): *THE NECESSARY DEATH OF A CHILD*

Now we move on to the second incident of the three in the story of Musa (a.s.) and Khidr (a.s.) in surah al-Kahf:

فَٱنطَلَقَا حَتَّىٰٓ إِذَا لَقِيَا غُلَٰمًا فَقَتَلَهُۥ قَالَ أَقَتَلْتَ نَفْسًا زَكِيَّةًۢ بِغَيْرِ نَفْسٍ لَّقَدْ جِئْتَ شَيْـًٔا نُّكْرًا ۝ قَالَ أَلَمْ أَقُل لَّكَ إِنَّكَ لَن تَسْتَطِيعَ مَعِىَ صَبْرًا ۝ قَالَ إِن سَأَلْتُكَ عَن شَىْءٍۭ بَعْدَهَا فَلَا تُصَٰحِبْنِى ۖ قَدْ بَلَغْتَ مِن لَّدُنِّى عُذْرًا ۝

"So they set out, until when they met a boy, al-Khidr (a.s.) killed him. [Musa] said, "Have you killed a pure soul for other than [having killed] a soul? You have certainly done a deplorable thing."

[Al-Khidr] said, "Did I not tell you that with me you would never be able to have patience?"

[Musa] said, "If I should ask you about anything after this, then do not keep me as a companion. You have obtained from me an excuse." (Al-Kahf 18:74-76)

Musa A.S: The Necessary Death of A Child

In the second incident, as they continued on their journey, they came across a child playing with other kids. Khidr (a.s.) goes to the child and kills him on the spot. Musa (a.s.) is of course horrified at this and blurts out in anger and shock, accusing Khidr (a.s.) of committing a grievous and heinous crime. The word used here is 'nukr' which means something really really terrible, as opposed to 'imr' in the first incident (the ship) which implies an evil of a lesser degree.

Khidr (a.s.) of course rebukes Musa (a.s.) because he once again forgot his promise to not ask anything until he was told about it. Musa (a.s.) realizing his mistake apologizes and tells Khidr (a.s.) that he will not do it again and that if he does it again, Khidr (a.s.) will then have an excuse to disallow him from following him further in his travels.

There are a few lessons here. First, this particular incident proves that Khidr (a.s.) was a prophet, for only a prophet could take somebody's life as commanded by Allah Jalla wa 'ala without any apparent reason. This is NOT allowed for anybody else in the world at any time or place. In Islam, the death penalty, or any other punishment for that matter, can only be meted out in light of strong evidence. Innocent until proven guilty is the axiom of Islamic Law.

Another interesting point is Musa's (a.s.) reaction to the situation. Just like in the first story about the boat, here too Musa (a.s.) was appalled and shocked at what Khidr (a.s.) did, and so he instantaneously, instinctively blurted out at the injustice that had occurred in front of his eyes. There is a very important lesson for us here, in that our conscience must never allow us to keep silent when we see an injustice happening. It should provoke a response from within us, either to do something with our hands if we are able, or with our tongues if the former is not possible, or at least hate such an act and pray against it.

This is in accordance with the hadith of Prophet (p.b.u.h.) on the authority of Abu Said al-Khudri:

> *"Whoever amongst you sees anything objectionable, let him change it with his hand, if he is not able, then with his tongue, and if he is not even able to do so, then with his heart, and the latter is the weakest form of faith."* [Muslim]

In today's world, a great sickness has befallen the ummah, where people rush to record with their smartphones a violent act they witness in front of their eyes and then quickly upload it onto YouTube to sensationalize it, instead of actually doing something about it or at least condemning it with their tongues and in their hearts.

Where in the past the race was to do something as quickly as possible to salvage the situation, now the race is to see who can upload the video fastest and get the most hits, completely oblivious to the predicament at hand.

May Allah save our hearts from becoming harder than rocks, lest we lose our ability to judge or worse, feel.

The main lesson of this incident is none other than the need to be patient in times of difficulty (just like in the previous incident), especially in a trial as great as losing a child. Khidr (a.s.) killed the child because Allah had informed him that this child would grow up to become a rebellious creature, who would not only bring doom to himself, but also to his parents by forcing them to leave Islam.

Some scholars say that the parents would turn to disbelief not because he would force them, but because their blind love for him would make them disobey Allah.

> *"And as for the boy, his parents were believers, and we feared that he would overburden them by transgression and disbelief. So we intended that their Lord should substitute for them one better than him in purity and nearer to mercy." (Al-Kahf 18:80-81)*

Losing a child is perhaps the most painful trial any person especially a mother, can experience. The prophet (p.b.u.h.) lost all his children before his death except Fatimah, who died soon after him. But there is great consolation for parents who lose their kids in the hadith below:

> *Abu Musa al-Ash'ari said: The Prophet said: "When the child of a man dies, Allah asks the*

angels, 'Did you take the soul of my slave's child?' They reply, 'Yes.' He asks them, 'Did you take away the apple of his eye?' And they reply, 'Yes.' Then He asks, 'What did My slave say?' They tell Him, 'He praised You and said, 'To Allah we belong and to Him is our return.' Allah says, 'Build a house for him in Paradise and call it Bait al-hamd (the house of Praise).'" [At- Tirmidhi, Hasan].

and this:

Jabir ibn 'Abdullah said, "I heard the Messenger of Allah, may Allah bless him and grant him peace, say, 'If anyone has three of his children die young and resigns them to Allah, he will enter the Garden.' We said, 'Messenger of Allah, what about two?' 'And two,' he said." Mahmud ibn Labid said to Jabir, "By Allah, I think that if you had asked, 'And one?' he would have given a similar answer." He said, "By Allah, I think so too." [Adab al-Mufrad, Hasan]

There are many other ahadith on this matter, but I think the two above would suffice for now. The key is to be patient and utter only good words when one loses a child, which is easier said than done. But if the grieving parents can do this, then how successful will they be in the Hereafter! At the death of his son Ibrahim, the Prophet (p.b.u.h.) wept and said these beautiful yet sad words:

> *"The eyes are shedding tears and the heart is grieved, and we will not say except what pleases our Lord, O Ibrahim ! Indeed we are grieved by your separation." [Bukhari]*

Verse 81 above says that Khidr (a.s.) wishes Allah would replace their loss with a child who is better. And so the implication here is that, when a child dies, either Allah will replace him/her with a better child, or the reward of the parents' suffering will be delayed until the Hereafter where the child would intercede for them to enter Jannah, insya Allah.

May Allah make us of those who are patient in the face of great calamities, so we obtain His mercy and reward, if not in this world, then the next insya-Allah.

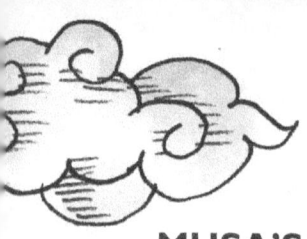

MUSA'S ENCOUNTER WITH KHIDR (PEACE BE UPON THEM BOTH): *THE RIGHTEOUS FATHER*

We now come to the last of the 3 incidents in the story of Nabi Musa (a.s.) and Khidr (a.s.).

فَٱنطَلَقَا حَتَّىٰٓ إِذَآ أَتَيَآ أَهۡلَ قَرۡيَةٍ ٱسۡتَطۡعَمَآ أَهۡلَهَا فَأَبَوۡاْ أَن يُضَيِّفُوهُمَا فَوَجَدَا فِيهَا جِدَارٗا يُرِيدُ أَن يَنقَضَّ فَأَقَامَهُۥۖ قَالَ لَوۡ شِئۡتَ لَتَّخَذۡتَ عَلَيۡهِ أَجۡرٗا ۝ قَالَ هَٰذَا فِرَاقُ بَيۡنِي وَبَيۡنِكَۚ سَأُنَبِّئُكَ بِتَأۡوِيلِ مَا لَمۡ تَسۡتَطِع عَّلَيۡهِ صَبۡرٗا ۝

So they set out, until when they came to the people of a town, they asked its people for food, but they refused to offer them hospitality. And they found therein a wall about to collapse, so al-Khidr (a.s.) restored it. [Musa] said, "If you wished, you could have taken for it a payment."

[Al-Khidr] said, "This is parting between me and you. I will inform you of the interpretation of that about which you could not have patience." (Al-Kahf 18: 77-78)

The first lesson in this incident is: It is the Sunnah of righteous people to treat their guests with utmost kindness. It was an unspoken rule in the time of the righteous predecessors that guests to a city or town must be given accommodation and good service for three days, with the most excellent service on the first day. The hadith of the Prophet in this regard is as follows:

> *Narrated by Abu Shuraih Al-Ka'bi: Allah's Apostle said: "Whosoever believes in Allah and the Last Day, should entertain his guest generously. The guest's reward is to provide him with a superior type of food for a night and a day, and a guest is to be entertained for three days, and whatever is offered beyond that, is regarded as something given in Sadaqa. And it is not lawful for a guest to stay with his host for such a long period as to put him in a critical position." [Sahih Bukhari]*

See how Rasulullah (p.b.u.h.) links kindness to guests with belief in Allah and the Day of Judgment. That is how important it is to treat guests with the best service. Unfortunately, in most parts of the world, we have become like the unkind and careless people in the story above whom Musa (a.s.) and Khidr (a.s.) encountered.

They refused to even give the two men food, let alone accommodation. May Allah protect us from miserliness and empower us to follow the sunnah of entertaining guests. Ameen.

Now back to the story. Musa (a.s.) was confused and perhaps a little bit frustrated at Khidr's (a.s.) misplaced kindness of repairing a dilapidated wall in the city without even asking for a reimbursement from the town's people. So Khidr (a.s.) now tells Musa (a.s.), the time for them to part has come.

Remember, it was Musa (a.s.) himself who placed the condition that Khidr (a.s.) can dismiss him if he asked another question. But before that of course, Khidr (a.s.) explains all the three events in sequence. We've done the first two, so let's go on to the explanation for this incident. Allah says:

$$\text{وَأَمَّا ٱلْجِدَارُ فَكَانَ لِغُلَٰمَيْنِ يَتِيمَيْنِ فِي ٱلْمَدِينَةِ وَكَانَ تَحْتَهُۥ كَنزٌ لَّهُمَا وَكَانَ أَبُوهُمَا صَٰلِحًا فَأَرَادَ رَبُّكَ أَن يَبْلُغَآ أَشُدَّهُمَا وَيَسْتَخْرِجَا كَنزَهُمَا رَحْمَةً مِّن رَّبِّكَ ۚ وَمَا فَعَلْتُهُۥ عَنْ أَمْرِى ۚ ذَٰلِكَ تَأْوِيلُ مَا لَمْ تَسْطِع عَّلَيْهِ صَبْرًا ﴿٨٢﴾}$$

"And as for the wall, it belonged to two orphan boys in the city, and there was beneath it a treasure for them, and their father had been righteous. So your Lord intended that they reach maturity and extract their treasure, as a mercy from your Lord. And I did it not of my own accord. That is the interpretation of that about which you could not have patience."" (Al-Kahf 18:82)

Musa A.S: The Righteous Father

The verse is self-explanatory I think. Allah wanted Khidr (a.s.) to repair the wall because beneath it was a treasure that a father had kept for his sons who were still very young. If the wall had collapsed completely, the townspeople whom we already know were very miserly, would have found it and taken it for themselves.

The two poor kids would never have had a chance of defending what was truly theirs. Thus the wall was repaired, so the two kids could take the treasure their father buried for them, upon attaining adulthood and full strength with which they would be able to defend their property.

The key point in this story is how Allah described the father. Allah described him as a righteous man (soliha). And so the lesson for us, especially those already with kids, is that, we need not worry too much about the future of our children after our death. Of course, we should not leave everything in the hands of Allah without doing anything all.

This is wrong and contradicts the message in the verse. The father did work hard and saved some money for his children so they could use it in future. But it was his righteousness which was of most benefit to his children, for Allah said it was because of his righteousness that Allah wished to show his children mercy, by restoring the wall through Prophet Khidr (a.s.) so the townspeople would not find the treasure he hid for his kids.

So dear parents and would be parents, if we want our kids to be under the shade of Allah's mercy, it is imperative for us first to be righteous people. There is no point if we worry too much about their future to the extent that we work and work and work, neglecting our duties towards Allah.

There is only loss in this kind of attitude. We lose our peace due to constant worry for our kids' future, and we lose Allah's mercy for them because we neglected His duties. May Allah make us fathers who are righteous, not only for our own benefit, but for the benefit of our progeny as well.

In this story too as in the previous two stories, the main theme and message is the importance of patience and tawakkul when facing difficult and inexplicable or strange situations. It is to place our trust in Allah and realize that Allah is in control of EVERYTHING.

Let us remember, that often there are things that happen which may seem unfair and puzzling to our minds, given our limited knowledge of how the qadar of Allah works. But Allah in His infinite wisdom decrees such events for a benefit, which may not be apparent immediately or even in this world, but will definitely become manifest in the Hereafter, provided we have patience and tawakkul i.e. we place our trust in Him and pray for the best.

With that, we conclude our limited discussion of the story of Musa (a.s.) and Khidr (a.s.). And all praise is due to Allah.

Note: I would like to point out an interesting aspect of the linguistic miracle of the Quran for those who know some Arabic. In verse 78, the verb 'not able' is used in its full form (istato'a), but in verse 82, after Khidr (a.s.) had explained all the puzzling events to Musa (a.s.), the same verb is now used without the letter 'ta' to make the pronunciation easier (isto'a), to suite the context, as if to say, just as Musa's (a.s.) confusion was eased after the explanation, so is the word simplified to make the reciter feel the peace of mind that had been obtained by Musa (a.s.) post-explanation. And Allah knows best.

SAYYIDINA ADAM (A.S) AND REPENTANCE

وَلَقَدْ خَلَقْنَـٰكُمْ ثُمَّ صَوَّرْنَـٰكُمْ ثُمَّ قُلْنَا لِلْمَلَـٰٓئِكَةِ ٱسْجُدُوا۟ لِـَٔادَمَ فَسَجَدُوٓا۟ إِلَّآ إِبْلِيسَ لَمْ يَكُن مِّنَ ٱلسَّـٰجِدِينَ ﴿١١﴾ قَالَ مَا مَنَعَكَ أَلَّا تَسْجُدَ إِذْ أَمَرْتُكَ ۖ قَالَ أَنَا۠ خَيْرٌ مِّنْهُ خَلَقْتَنِى مِن نَّارٍ وَخَلَقْتَهُۥ مِن طِينٍ ﴿١٢﴾ قَالَ فَٱهْبِطْ مِنْهَا فَمَا يَكُونُ لَكَ أَن تَتَكَبَّرَ فِيهَا فَٱخْرُجْ إِنَّكَ مِنَ ٱلصَّـٰغِرِينَ ﴿١٣﴾ قَالَ أَنظِرْنِىٓ إِلَىٰ يَوْمِ يُبْعَثُونَ ﴿١٤﴾ قَالَ إِنَّكَ مِنَ ٱلْمُنظَرِينَ ﴿١٥﴾ قَالَ فَبِمَآ أَغْوَيْتَنِى لَأَقْعُدَنَّ لَهُمْ صِرَٰطَكَ ٱلْمُسْتَقِيمَ ﴿١٦﴾ ثُمَّ لَـَٔاتِيَنَّهُم مِّنۢ بَيْنِ أَيْدِيهِمْ وَمِنْ خَلْفِهِمْ وَعَنْ أَيْمَـٰنِهِمْ وَعَن شَمَآئِلِهِمْ ۖ وَلَا تَجِدُ أَكْثَرَهُمْ شَـٰكِرِينَ ﴿١٧﴾ قَالَ ٱخْرُجْ مِنْهَا مَذْءُومًا مَّدْحُورًا ۖ لَّمَن تَبِعَكَ مِنْهُمْ لَأَمْلَأَنَّ جَهَنَّمَ مِنكُمْ أَجْمَعِينَ ﴿١٨﴾ وَيَـٰٓـَٔادَمُ ٱسْكُنْ أَنتَ وَزَوْجُكَ ٱلْجَنَّةَ فَكُلَا مِنْ حَيْثُ شِئْتُمَا وَلَا تَقْرَبَا هَـٰذِهِ ٱلشَّجَرَةَ فَتَكُونَا مِنَ ٱلظَّـٰلِمِينَ ﴿١٩﴾ فَوَسْوَسَ لَهُمَا ٱلشَّيْطَـٰنُ لِيُبْدِىَ لَهُمَا مَا وُۥرِىَ عَنْهُمَا مِن سَوْءَٰتِهِمَا وَقَالَ مَا نَهَىٰكُمَا رَبُّكُمَا عَنْ هَـٰذِهِ ٱلشَّجَرَةِ إِلَّآ أَن تَكُونَا مَلَكَيْنِ أَوْ تَكُونَا مِنَ ٱلْخَـٰلِدِينَ ﴿٢٠﴾ وَقَاسَمَهُمَآ إِنِّى لَكُمَا لَمِنَ ٱلنَّـٰصِحِينَ ﴿٢١﴾ فَدَلَّىٰهُمَا بِغُرُورٍ ۚ فَلَمَّا ذَاقَا ٱلشَّجَرَةَ بَدَتْ لَهُمَا سَوْءَٰتُهُمَا وَطَفِقَا

يَخْصِفَانِ عَلَيْهِمَا مِن وَرَقِ ٱلْجَنَّةِ ۖ وَنَادَىٰهُمَا رَبُّهُمَا أَلَمْ أَنْهَكُمَا عَن تِلْكُمَا ٱلشَّجَرَةِ وَأَقُل لَّكُمَا إِنَّ ٱلشَّيْطَانَ لَكُمَا عَدُوٌّ مُّبِينٌ ۝ قَالَا رَبَّنَا ظَلَمْنَا أَنفُسَنَا وَإِن لَّمْ تَغْفِرْ لَنَا وَتَرْحَمْنَا لَنَكُونَنَّ مِنَ ٱلْخَٰسِرِينَ ۝ قَالَ ٱهْبِطُوا۟ بَعْضُكُمْ لِبَعْضٍ عَدُوٌّ ۖ وَلَكُمْ فِى ٱلْأَرْضِ مُسْتَقَرٌّ وَمَتَٰعٌ إِلَىٰ حِينٍ ۝ قَالَ فِيهَا تَحْيَوْنَ وَفِيهَا تَمُوتُونَ وَمِنْهَا تُخْرَجُونَ ۝ يَٰبَنِى ءَادَمَ قَدْ أَنزَلْنَا عَلَيْكُمْ لِبَاسًا يُوَٰرِى سَوْءَٰتِكُمْ وَرِيشًا ۖ وَلِبَاسُ ٱلتَّقْوَىٰ ذَٰلِكَ خَيْرٌ ۚ ذَٰلِكَ مِنْ ءَايَٰتِ ٱللَّهِ لَعَلَّهُمْ يَذَّكَّرُونَ ۝ يَٰبَنِى ءَادَمَ لَا يَفْتِنَنَّكُمُ ٱلشَّيْطَٰنُ كَمَا أَخْرَجَ أَبَوَيْكُم مِّنَ ٱلْجَنَّةِ يَنزِعُ عَنْهُمَا لِبَاسَهُمَا لِيُرِيَهُمَا سَوْءَٰتِهِمَآ ۗ إِنَّهُۥ يَرَىٰكُمْ هُوَ وَقَبِيلُهُۥ مِنْ حَيْثُ لَا تَرَوْنَهُمْ ۗ إِنَّا جَعَلْنَا ٱلشَّيَٰطِينَ أَوْلِيَآءَ لِلَّذِينَ لَا يُؤْمِنُونَ ۝

"And We have certainly created you, [O mankind], and given you [human] form. Then We said to the angels, "Prostrate to Adam"; so they prostrated, except for Iblis. He was not of those who prostrated. [Allāh] said, "What prevented you from prostrating when I commanded you?"

[Iblis] said, "I am better than him. You created me from fire and created him from clay [i.e., earth]." [Allāh] said, "Descend from it [i.e., Paradise], for it is not for you to be arrogant therein. So get out;

indeed, you are of the debased."

[Iblīs] said, "Reprieve me until the Day they are resurrected." [Allāh] said, "Indeed, you are of those reprieved." [Iblīs] said, "Because You have put me in error, I will surely sit in wait for them [i.e., mankind] on Your straight path. Then I will come to them from before them and from behind them and on their right and on their left, and You will not find most of them grateful [to You]."

[Allāh] said, "Depart from it [i.e., Paradise], reproached and expelled. Whoever follows you among them – I will surely fill Hell with you, all together." And "O Adam, dwell, you and your wife, in Paradise and eat from wherever you will but do not approach this tree, lest you be among the wrongdoers."

But Iblīs whispered to them to make apparent to them that which was concealed from them of their private parts. He said, "Your Lord did not forbid you this tree except that you become angels or become of the immortal." And he swore [by Allāh] to them, "Indeed, I am to you from among the sincere advisors."

So he made them fall, through deception. And when they tasted of the tree, their private parts became apparent to them, and they began to *fasten together over themselves from the leaves of Paradise. And their Lord called to them, "Did I not forbid you from that tree and tell you that Iblis is to you a clear enemy?"*

They said, "Our Lord, we have wronged ourselves, and if You do not forgive us and have mercy upon us, we will surely be among the losers." [Allāh] said, "Descend, being to one another enemies. And for you on the earth is a place of settlement and enjoyment [i.e., provision] for a time." He said, "Therein you will live, and therein you will die, and from it you will be brought forth."

O children of Adam, We have bestowed upon you clothing to conceal your private parts and as adornment. But the clothing of righteousness – that is best. That is from the signs of Allāh that perhaps they will remember.

O children of Adam, let not Iblis tempt you as he removed your parents from Paradise, stripping them of their clothing to show them their private parts. Indeed, he sees you, he and his tribe, from where you do not see them. Indeed, We have made the devils allies to those who do not believe." (Al-A'raf 7: 11-27)

Sayyidina Adam (A.S) and Repentance

We all know that Adam (a.s.) was the first person created by Allah jalla wa 'ala and that he lived in Jannah with his wife Hawwa for a period of time. Right after he was created, Allah ordered the angels along with Iblis the Jinn, who was amongst the angels, to prostrate before Adam (a.s.). They all prostrated except for Iblis because he felt he was superior since he was created from fire while Adam (a.s.) was created from clay.

Thus, Iblis was the first 'racist' to exist in the universe. He felt himself to be better than Adam just because he was made of something he thought to be superior. Because he refused to prostrate before Adam, Allah cursed him and banished him from Jannah. But before he left, he asked Allah to give him respite until the Day of Judgment and Allah granted him that request so he could mislead as many of the children of Adam as possible because he felt Adam was the cause of his banishment from Jannah.

So what did he do? He plotted a plot to get Adam (a.s.) and his wife out of Jannah too. Allah had told them to eat whatever they wanted in Jannah except for the fruit from the forbidden tree. But Iblis whispered evil thoughts into their hearts and minds, promising them with a false promise, that if they ate the fruit from the forbidden tree, they would become immortal.

After whispering and whispering many times, Adam (a.s.) and his wife fell for his trick and ate the forbidden fruit. At once, their clothes disappeared from their bodies and they quickly started covering themselves up with the leaves of Jannah. That was what Iblis wanted all along! To expose their private parts. And this is what he continues to do to this day i.e. turn people naked even though they have plenty of clothes to wear! Iblis loves shamelessness and that is the first consequence of Adam (a.s.) following his advice.

Then what happened? Allah banished Adam (a.s.) and his wife from Jannah because they disobeyed His command. So you see what Iblis did there? He provoked them towards a minor disobedience namely eating a forbidden fruit, which resulted in them becoming naked and hence their removal from Jannah. That is how he tricked our Father, and that is how he continues to trick all of us because he wants none of us to enter Jannah but instead rot in the Fire of Hell with him.

He whispers into our minds to do small acts of disobedience, which get bigger and bigger, not infrequently leading to sins which are related to nakedness or shamelessness – whether it be through our speech or actions – and ultimately our disqualification from entering Jannah, for Jannah is only fit for those who obey their Lord and guard their chastity with the beautiful clothes Allah has bestowed upon us.

Now what happens after Adam (a.s.) and his wife were banished from Jannah is what makes this story so intriguing. Both Adam (a.s.) and Iblis disobeyed Allah. Both were banished from Jannah as a result. The difference though is that Iblis blamed Allah for misleading him, whereas Adam (a.s.) and his wife admitted their mistake and repented. Iblis was arrogant, while Adam (a.s.) was humble. And because of that, he was forgiven and shall enter Jannah again, while Iblis will remain cursed forever until he enters the Fire of Hell.

So the main moral of this story is, we should always admit our mistakes and repent to Allah for Allah loves those who repent, since it is a manifestation of our humility and dependence on him. On the flipside, Allah dislikes those who are arrogant and worse, blame others when they have committed a mistake because of their arrogance. Indeed Allah despises those who are arrogant. And Allah has placed the love of humility and hate for arrogance even in the hearts of man. So if we are humble and admit our mistakes, not only will Allah love us but the people around us will love us too.

On the other hand, if we are arrogant and always blame others for our own mistakes, not only will we be cursed by Allah, but also the people around us and the rest of creation.

It should be noted too, that the nature of the sins committed by Iblis and Adam (a.s) were different. Iblis disobeyed Allah out of arrogance, while Adam disobeyed Allah because of weakness. So arrogance is a dangerous trait, because not only does it make us disobey Allah, it makes us far removed from His mercy thereafter as Allah blackens our hearts so we refuse to admit our mistakes and commit further sins. But if we commit a sin because of weakness, then Allah is Most Forgiving provided we quickly turn to him in repentance.

May Allah make us repentant sinners like our Father Adam (a.s.), and may He protect us from being arrogant sinners like Iblis.

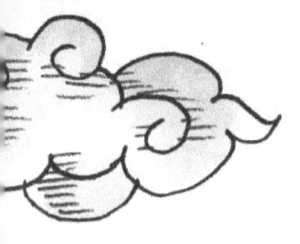

SAYYIDINA NUH'S (A.S.) EXHORTATION TO SEEK FORGIVENESS

فَقُلْتُ ٱسْتَغْفِرُوا رَبَّكُمْ إِنَّهُۥ كَانَ غَفَّارًا ۝ يُرْسِلِ ٱلسَّمَآءَ عَلَيْكُم مِّدْرَارًا ۝ وَيُمْدِدْكُم بِأَمْوَٰلٍ وَبَنِينَ وَيَجْعَل لَّكُمْ جَنَّٰتٍ وَيَجْعَل لَّكُمْ أَنْهَٰرًا ۝

I said, "Ask forgiveness of your Lord. Truly He is Endlessly Forgiving.

He will send [rain from] the sky upon you in [continuing] showers

and reinforce you with more wealth and sons, and grant you gardens and grant you waterways.

(Nuh 71:10-12)

We all know how asking for forgiveness erases our sins and that Allah loves those who seek forgiveness. But what is the manifestation of Allah's love for the servant who makes istighfar (seek forgiveness)? This exhortation of Sayyidina Nuh (a.s.) gives us a glimpse of that love.

Allah loves those who seek forgiveness so much, that not only He forgives their sins, He increases them in all sorts of blessings without them having to even ask for it! The blessings mentioned in these verses are few, but they represent the totality of blessings that all men covet.

A great scholar of the past, Imam Hassan Al-Basri, was approached by a few people with different problems from poverty to having no children. To all of them, his advice was, "Seek forgiveness from Allah."

A student of the Imam asked him why he gave the same response to all of them despite their varying problems, to which the great Imam replied, "I have not said anything of my own accord, but Allah said in surah Nuh …" *[and he recited the verses above]* (Tafsir al-Qurtubiy).

Such is the power of making istighfar. Not only will our sins be forgiven, Allah will also shower upon us many blessings beyond what we can ever hope and imagine.

Let us be of those who always say Astaghfirullah, Astaghfirullah that we may receive the abundant blessings therein that Allah has promised. Ameen.

SAYYIDINA IBRAHIM (A.S.) AND THE NOBLE GUESTS

هَلْ أَتَىٰكَ حَدِيثُ ضَيْفِ إِبْرَٰهِيمَ ٱلْمُكْرَمِينَ ۝ إِذْ دَخَلُوا۟ عَلَيْهِ فَقَالُوا۟ سَلَٰمًۭا ۖ قَالَ سَلَٰمٌۭ قَوْمٌۭ مُّنكَرُونَ ۝ فَرَاغَ إِلَىٰٓ أَهْلِهِۦ فَجَآءَ بِعِجْلٍۢ سَمِينٍۢ ۝ فَقَرَّبَهُۥٓ إِلَيْهِمْ قَالَ أَلَا تَأْكُلُونَ ۝

Has there reached you the story of the honored guests of Abraham?

When they entered upon him and said, "[We greet you with] peace." He answered, "[And upon you] peace; [you are] a people unknown."

Then he went to his family and came with a fat [roasted] calf

And placed it near them; he said, "Will you not eat?" (Adh-Dhaariyaat 51:24-27)

This story in the Quran about Ibrahim (a.s.) and his guests is the epitome of how we should treat our guests. Allah had sent a few angels in the form of men to the house of Ibrahim to give him glad tidings of a son (Sayyidina Ishaq (a.s.)) on their way to the destroy the people of Sayyidina Lut (a.s.).

Of course, Ibrahim (a.s.) did not at first know they were angels. They greeted him with the greetings of peace (Salaaman) and he replied with the same greeting (Salaamun). Scholars say although both greetings are the same, the form Ibrahim used to reply the angels with the ending 'mun' instead of 'man' is more emphatic. So there's our first lesson i.e. to respond to a greeting with something better than what was given. This is in accordance with Allah's command in surah An-Nisa' verse 86:

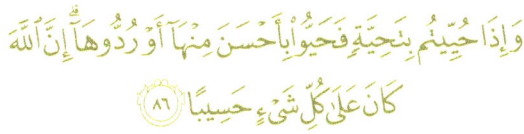

And when you are greeted with a greeting, greet [in return] with one better than it or [at least] return it [in a like manner]. Indeed Allāh is ever, over all things, an Accountant.

So next time somebody greets us with 'Assalamu 'alaykum', we should reply with 'Wa alaykum as-salam warahmatullah' or at least the same. Something so simple in our eyes, but often overlooked, yet Allah takes account of it, as stated at the end of the verse.

After Ibrahim (a.s.) greeted them, he invited them in even though he did not know who they were. Because they greeted him with the greeting of peace, he assumed the best of them. Perhaps they were travellers, who just wanted a place to rest. Or maybe they were a people from a different

place who wanted to seek counsel from him knowing that he was a messenger of God. In any case, he allowed them in, and before long, quickly rushed to his family to prepare a meal for his guests. And not just any meal, but the best he could give, a fat roasted calf! Subhanallah!

Upon preparing the calf, he, being the exemplary host he was, placed it right in front of them so they didn't have to get up from their seats to take the food. How amazing is that?

And when they did not touch the food, he was quick to ask them, "Will you not eat?" most likely out of concern that they may not like the food. This sort of beautiful etiquette was something that our elders were particular about, but is waning in our generation. I personally would usually ask any guests if they would like something to drink, but my mother would be enraged if I did that.

"Don't ask them if they want a drink, but ask them what drink they would like!" she would say.

You can read the rest of the story in the Quran, but I will stop here because it was this aspect of the story namely Sayyidina Ibrahim's (a.s.) exemplary treatment of his guests, that I wanted to highlight. May Allah help us to emulate him the next time we receive our guests. Ameen.

Note: One should also supplement knowledge of how Rasulullah (p.b.u.h.) received his guests to complement the points in this Quranic story.

SAYYIDINA YA'KUB (A.S.) AND THE TEARS OF SADNESS

وَتَوَلَّىٰ عَنْهُمْ وَقَالَ يَٰأَسَفَىٰ عَلَىٰ يُوسُفَ وَٱبْيَضَّتْ عَيْنَاهُ مِنَ ٱلْحُزْنِ فَهُوَ كَظِيمٌ ۝ قَالُوا۟ تَٱللَّهِ تَفْتَؤُا۟ تَذْكُرُ يُوسُفَ حَتَّىٰ تَكُونَ حَرَضًا أَوْ تَكُونَ مِنَ ٱلْهَٰلِكِينَ ۝ قَالَ إِنَّمَآ أَشْكُوا۟ بَثِّى وَحُزْنِىٓ إِلَى ٱللَّهِ وَأَعْلَمُ مِنَ ٱللَّهِ مَا لَا تَعْلَمُونَ ۝

And he turned away from them and said, "Oh, my sorrow over Yusof," and his eyes became white from grief, for he was [of that] a suppressor.

They said, "By Allāh, you will not cease remembering Yusof until you become fatally ill or become of those who perish."

He said, "I only complain of my suffering and my grief to Allāh, and I know from Allāh that which you do not know. (Yusof 12: 84-86)

These verses are taken from the very famous story of Sayyidina Yusof (a.s.) in Surah Yusof, the twelfth Surah of the Quran. This is the part where the sons of Ya'kub (a.s.), the father of Yusof (a.s.),

Sayyidina Ya'kub (A.S) and the Tears of Sadness

came back from Egypt without the youngest of them, Binyamin, after meeting Yusof (a.s.) because he was held captive for the alleged crime of stealing the King's cup (of course this was a plot by Yusof (a.s.) himself with his brother to bring their father to Egypt).

The reason I've highlighted this part of the story is to show how much Sayydina Ya'kub (a.s.) cried out of sadness at the loss of and the yearning to see both his sons, especially Yusof (a.s.). He cried so much that he turned blind, and his family were fed up of his mourning.

Their reaction was quite understandable given that he was still mourning and crying over the loss of Yusof (a.s.) after all these years (more than 30 years had passed)! He however said to them that he only complains of his grief to Allah and knows something from Allah which they do not know.

In our society, sometimes we are quick to judge people who mourn a loss, who cry a lot, as being impatient. But we should let them be, for the pain of separation is severe. Let them cry as Sayyidina Ya'kub (a.s.) did until he became blind. This pressure to remain strong and composed is especially difficult for men, who are expected to be macho in the face of adversity and loss.

But crying, as we can see in the story above, is not a sign of weakness but in fact the most natural thing in the world, even if you're a man. Do not cry if you do not want to, but don't judge others as being weak or impatient if they cry. Even Rasulullah (p.b.u.h.) cried when he suffered the loss of friends and family. He cried so much that tears would fall from his beard!

The important thing when mourning and crying though, is to complain TO Allah as Ya'kub (a.s.) did, and not complain ABOUT Allah, as many of us do when harm touches us. "Why me?", "How can God punish me like this?", "What did I do to deserve this?" are expressions that should be avoided as they show a lack of trust in the will of God.

When the beloved son of Rasulullah (p.b.u.h.), Ibrahim, died at a tender age of about 18 months, the Prophet cried and uttered such beautiful and profound words as recorded in Sahih Bukhari:

Narrated by Anas bin Malik:

We went with Allah's Messenger (p.b.u.h.) to the blacksmith Abu Saif, and he was the husband of the wet-nurse of Ibrahim (the son of the Prophet). Allah's Messenger took Ibrahim and kissed him and smelled him and later we entered Abu Saif's house and at that time Ibrahim was in his last breaths, and the eyes of Allah's Messenger (p.b.u.h.) started shedding tears. `Abdur Rahman bin `Auf said, "O Allah's Apostle, even you are weeping!" He said, "O Ibn `Auf, this is mercy." Then he wept more and *said, "The eyes are shedding tears and the heart is grieved, and we will not say except what pleases our Lord, O Ibrahim ! Indeed we are grieved by your separation."*

So the next time we see someone cry, cut them some slack and let them be. Allah recorded the story of Sayyidina Ya'kub (a.s.) crying until he turned blind as a lesson for us so we do not become judgmental about people who cry when in sorrow, even if they were men.

Remember though, we should always advise each other to complain to Allah about our sorrows as he did, and not complain about Allah.

SAYYIDINA YUSOF (A.S.) AND THE GRAND DESIGN OF ALLAH

وَقَالَ ٱلَّذِى ٱشْتَرَىٰهُ مِن مِّصْرَ لِٱمْرَأَتِهِۦٓ أَكْرِمِى مَثْوَىٰهُ عَسَىٰٓ أَن يَنفَعَنَآ أَوْ نَتَّخِذَهُۥ وَلَدًا ۚ وَكَذَٰلِكَ مَكَّنَّا لِيُوسُفَ فِى ٱلْأَرْضِ وَلِنُعَلِّمَهُۥ مِن تَأْوِيلِ ٱلْأَحَادِيثِ ۚ وَٱللَّهُ غَالِبٌ عَلَىٰٓ أَمْرِهِۦ وَلَٰكِنَّ أَكْثَرَ ٱلنَّاسِ لَا يَعْلَمُونَ ۝

"The Egyptian who had bought him told his wife, 'Look after him with honour and respect. It's possible he will be of use to us or perhaps we might adopt him as a son.' And thus We established Yusof in the land to teach him the true meaning of events. Allah is in control of His affair. However, most of mankind do not know." [Yusof 12: 21]

The story of Sayyidina Yusof (a.s.) is the most beautiful of all the prophetic stories in the Quran, not least because it is the only story told from start to finish coherently in a single surah namely surah Yusof.

There are many gems to be learnt from this story but we will focus on one theme of this surah, which is perhaps the main theme, namely Allah is in complete control of all the things that occur in our lives and that He works in the most subtle of ways, often beyond our wildest imagination.

Prophet Yusof (a.s.) underwent a multitude of trials in his life from the time he was a child all the way until he was released from prison in Egypt. Perhaps the most painful of these tribulations was how his own brothers treated him. They were jealous of him because they felt their father, Sayydina Ya'kub (a.s.), loved him more than them.

As a result they plotted to kill him, but decided to commit a lesser evil by throwing him, at the time only about 6 or 7 years old, into a deep abandoned well, hoping some caravan would pick him up and take him to a faraway land from where he would never come back.

He was then picked up by a caravan and sold as a slave for a miserable price to a minister in Egypt, hundreds of miles away from his home in Palestine (Canaan).

He grew up in the house of the minister into a supremely handsome young man. He was so handsome that the wife of the minister fell in love and flirted with him. When he refused to reciprocate, she together with her lady friends who also lusted for him – they were so consumed by his handsomeness that they cut their hands while they were slicing fruits when they saw him pass them by – plotted to put him in jail and they succeeded.

He stayed in jail for a long time until the king of Egypt released him because he managed to interpret the king's dream. When he took charge of the storehouses of the land, he managed to save food not just for the people of Egypt but also for the people of neighbouring lands.

This then led to his brothers coming to get food from him and after the discovery that Yusof (a.s.) was still alive, Allah reunited the whole family in Egypt, after at least 30 long years of separation.

This story is so amazing because although Sayyidina Yusof (a.s.) suffered the evil plots of people including his own brothers throughout his life, all of those plots resided within the grand plan of Allah for him. In fact, it is because of their plots that he became what he became. The evil ones plotted, intending evil for Yusof (a.s.), but Allah plotted too, and in the end, their evil plots only served to fulfill the grand design that Allah had for Yusof (a.s.).

Of course Sayyidina Yusof (a.s.) could have never guessed that all the suffering he faced would pave his way towards greatness, but such is how Allah works, with subtlety. The important thing is for us to realize that Allah is in complete control of everything that happens in the universe, and that He executes His grand plan with absolute subtlety.

It is we who must be patient in times of difficulty and never lose hope, but instead place our trust in Allah, in Whose Hand rests the decree of all matters. Hence the words of Sayyidina Yusof (a.s.) when Allah reunited him with his family in Egypt:

$$وَرَفَعَ أَبَوَيْهِ عَلَى الْعَرْشِ وَخَرُّوا لَهُ سُجَّدًا ۖ وَقَالَ يَا أَبَتِ هَٰذَا تَأْوِيلُ رُؤْيَايَ مِن قَبْلُ قَدْ جَعَلَهَا رَبِّي حَقًّا ۖ وَقَدْ أَحْسَنَ بِي إِذْ أَخْرَجَنِي مِنَ السِّجْنِ وَجَاءَ بِكُم مِّنَ الْبَدْوِ مِن بَعْدِ أَن نَّزَغَ الشَّيْطَانُ بَيْنِي وَبَيْنَ إِخْوَتِي ۚ إِنَّ رَبِّي لَطِيفٌ لِّمَا يَشَاءُ ۚ إِنَّهُ هُوَ الْعَلِيمُ الْحَكِيمُ ﴿١٠٠﴾$$

"And he raised his parents upon the throne, and they bowed to him in prostration. And he said, "O my father, this is the explanation of my vision of before. My Lord has made it reality. And He was certainly good to me when He took me out of prison and brought you [here] from bedouin life after Iblis had induced [estrangement] between me and my brothers. Indeed, my Lord is Subtle in what He wills. Indeed, it is He who is the Knowing, the Wise."

[Yusof 12: 100]

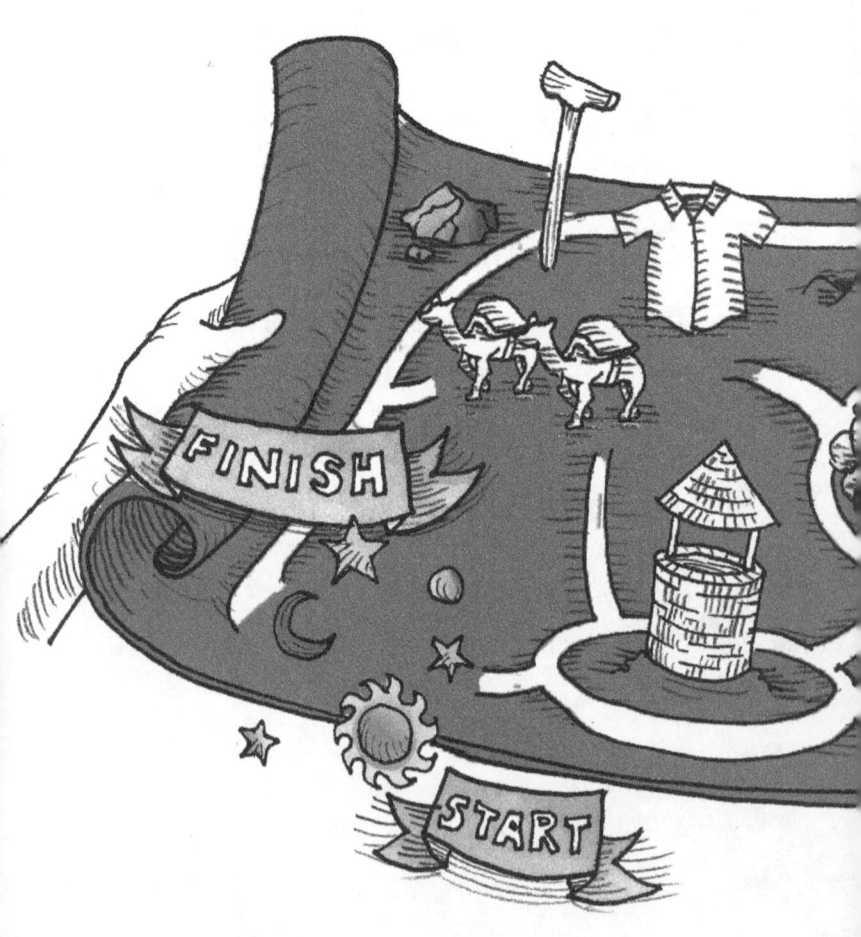

SAYYIDINA DAAWOOD AND THE JUDGMENT OF HIS SON (PEACE BE UPON THEM BOTH)

وَدَاوُۥدَ وَسُلَيْمَٰنَ إِذْ يَحْكُمَانِ فِى ٱلْحَرْثِ إِذْ نَفَشَتْ فِيهِ غَنَمُ ٱلْقَوْمِ وَكُنَّا لِحُكْمِهِمْ شَٰهِدِينَ ۝ فَفَهَّمْنَٰهَا سُلَيْمَٰنَ ۚ وَكُلًّا ءَاتَيْنَا حُكْمًا وَعِلْمًا ۚ وَسَخَّرْنَا مَعَ دَاوُۥدَ ٱلْجِبَالَ يُسَبِّحْنَ وَٱلطَّيْرَ ۚ وَكُنَّا فَٰعِلِينَ ۝

"And [mention] Dawood and Sulaiman, when they judged concerning the field – when the sheep of a people overran it [at night], and We were witness to their judgement. And We gave understanding of it [i.e., the case] to Sulaiman, and to each [of them] We gave judgement and knowledge. And We subjected the mountains to exalt [Us], along with Dawood and [also] the birds. And We were doing [that]." (Al-Anbiya' 21:78-79)

This is an interesting story in the Quran about a case that was brought before Prophet Dawood and his son (peace be upon them). We know that Dawood (a.s.) was a king and naturally the chief judge of his people. His son, Prophet Sulaiman (a.s.) was of course

Sayyidina Daawood and the Judgment of His Son

the crown prince and most likely sat with his father when there were cases to judge.

Now a person came to them about an issue. His grapes were eaten by the sheep of another person at night while they were asleep. So there was some negligence on the part of the sheep owner. After listening to the case, Dawood (a.s.) judged that the sheep owner should hand over some of his sheep to the owner of the grapes as compensation.

Sulaiman (a.s.) who was present during the hearing said, "Not like this". The father then asked, "How then?" So Sulaiman (a.s.) said, "Give the grapes to the owner of the sheep and let him tend them until they grow back as they were, and give the sheep to the owner of the grapes and let him benefit from them until the grapes have grown back as they were. Then the grapes should be given back to their owner, and the sheep should be given back to their owner." *[Tafseer of Ibn Kathir]*

See how the son felt comfortable to voice his opinion and how the father accepted that opinion. Both were prophets, but Dawood (a.s.) was the king at the time and was probably much wiser given his vast experience. Despite that, he did not arrogantly dismiss his son's opinion.

The fact that the son could express what he felt about the case shows that Dawood (a.s.) was a very kind and

Sayyidina Daawood and the Judgment of His Son

wise king who was very willing to receive advice and in fact encouraged people to speak up if they had something on their mind, like the Queen of Sheba in Surah An-Naml (The Ants). Truly, a mark of a great ruler.

Indeed, Allah says that He gave Sulaiman (a.s.) a better understanding of the case, hence, the better judgment, but He the Most High did not condemn Dawood's (a.s.) decision but instead reiterated that to both of them He gave knowledge and wisdom.

What we learn from this story is that, first of all, all understanding is from Allah. We should not be too proud if we make a good decision, but instead should thank Allah for guiding us to make the right decision.

Secondly, we should be humble regardless of our status and age. It is this humility – which can only arise if we internalize the first point that all knowledge, understanding and wisdom is from Allah – that will enable us to be open to advice and criticism of our judgments and decisions.

And thirdly, we should bear in mind that if we make a decision after weighing the pros and cons properly and it turns out to be the wrong decision, then Allah will not punish us for that because we did our best and are only human. No doubt, we can only make a good decision if Allah wills for such a thing to happen. As Prophet Muhammad (p.b.u.h.) said:

"If the judge does his best, studies the case and reaches the right conclusion, he will have two rewards. If he does his best, studies the case and reaches the wrong conclusion, he will have one reward." [Bukhari]

May Allah help us to be humble like Prophet Dawood (a.s.), especially those of us in positions of power, so people around us are comfortable to express any disagreements or opinions and so that we accept criticism and advice with open hearts. For verily, all knowledge and understanding is from Allah, not from ourselves. There really is no need to be proud!

SAYYIDINA SULAIMAN (A.S.) AND THE ANTS

حَتَّىٰٓ إِذَآ أَتَوْا۟ عَلَىٰ وَادِ ٱلنَّمْلِ قَالَتْ نَمْلَةٌ يَـٰٓأَيُّهَا ٱلنَّمْلُ ٱدْخُلُوا۟ مَسَـٰكِنَكُمْ لَا يَحْطِمَنَّكُمْ سُلَيْمَـٰنُ وَجُنُودُهُۥ وَهُمْ لَا يَشْعُرُونَ ۝ فَتَبَسَّمَ ضَاحِكًا مِّن قَوْلِهَا وَقَالَ رَبِّ أَوْزِعْنِىٓ أَنْ أَشْكُرَ نِعْمَتَكَ ٱلَّتِىٓ أَنْعَمْتَ عَلَىَّ وَعَلَىٰ وَٰلِدَىَّ وَأَنْ أَعْمَلَ صَـٰلِحًا تَرْضَىٰهُ وَأَدْخِلْنِى بِرَحْمَتِكَ فِى عِبَادِكَ ٱلصَّـٰلِحِينَ ۝

And gathered for Sulaiman were his soldiers of the jinn and men and birds, and they were [marching] in rows, Until, when they came upon the valley of the ants, an ant said, "O ants, enter your dwellings that you not be crushed by Sulaiman and his soldiers while they perceive not." So [Sulaiman] smiled, amused at her speech, and said, "My Lord, enable me to be grateful for Your favor which You have bestowed upon me and upon my parents and to do righteousness of which You approve. And admit me by Your mercy into [the ranks of] Your righteous servants." (An-Naml 27:17-19)

This story is for me the best example of how man's relationship with nature should be. Sulaiman (a.s.) and his armies were marching until they came to a valley of ants. When the ants saw them approaching, one of the ants implored the other ants to quickly enter their nest lest they be trampled upon by the army without them realizing it.

The last part of that verse, 'while they perceive not', is key to understanding the verse properly. The ant could have just stopped short of mentioning that last part, but it was mentioned nonetheless for an important purpose.

The implication of the verse is that the armies would only trample on the ants if they did not realize the ants were there. If they did, they would not trample on them. Such is nature's expectation of the righteous. They are expected to care for nature and not cause her harm without just cause. We are not even supposed to step on an ant for no reason if we can see it, let alone destroy whole forests and oceans because of our insatiable appetite and greed.

Everything in the universe is a sign of God and all are in constant praise and glorification of Him.

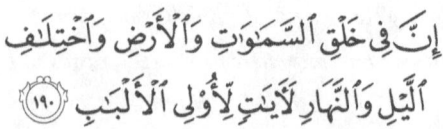

"Indeed, in the creation of the heavens and the earth and the alternation of the night and the day

Sayyidina Sulaiman (A.S) and the Ants

are signs for those of understanding." (Ali 'Imran 3:190)

Whatever is in the heavens and whatever is on the earth exalts Allāh, and He is the Exalted in Might, the Wise. (As-Saff 61:1)

Thus, we have no right to destroy anything of the creation without purpose because the creation is constantly making tasbih of Allah. It is bad enough that we are slack in remembering Allah, so at least we should let the creation live in peace and continue their tasbih of Allah.

But no, we throw rubbish everywhere, we pollute the environment, we cut down forests, we consume far more than we need, we cannot be bothered to recycle or reuse and and and…… We are selfish and do not have an iota of shame or guilt in the way we interact with the environment.

If we claim to be Muslims and khulafa' of Allah, then we must care for the environment since that is what the 'alam (nature) expects of us, as per the words of the ant.

It is this realization that caused Sulaiman (a.s.) to smile in amusement, and make a dua' so Allah grants him the strength to be grateful for all the blessings Allah has given him and his parents and to do righteous deeds, which naturally and perhaps particularly in this context, includes guarding the 'alam to the best of his ability. Say ameen!

ABOUT THE AUTHOR

Aqtar Mohamed Ummar graduated from the University of Edinburgh with a medical degree in 2012. After working as a doctor for a very short time, he resigned and decided to pursue his passion in teaching. He taught in two government schools for about a year and half as a substitute teacher before pursuing a master's degree in Integrative Neuroscience at Edinburgh University also. Upon return from Edinburgh, he was offered a job as Chemistry and Biology teacher at KMSS. Currently, he is Head of Academic Division and teaches Islamiyyat and Biology at IGCSE level, apart from being a tutor for the tahfiz program. This is his first book published by Yayasan Pendidikan Khalifah, after "Reviving the Spirit of Ramadan: Beyond Do's and Don'ts" (as translator) published by Abideen Books. He can be contacted at aqtarmohamed@gmail.com.

THANK YOU FOR PURCHASING THIS BOOK. SO, WHAT'S NEXT?

As a token of appreciation, we would like to give you a **FREE AUDIO** of this book, so that you can enjoy the content of this book while driving, jogging, relaxing at home or in any way you prefer.

Please go to **tinyletter.com/abideenbooks** and leave your e-mail there. We will deliver the audio right into your inbox.

If you are interested to **generate some side income** by becoming our **AFFILIATE AGENT**, please register at **bit.ly/bukuaqtar**

MAY ALLAH MAKE THIS BOOK BENEFICIAL FOR YOU!

If you have any feedback or inquiry about this book, you may contact directly at aqtarmohamed@gmail.com or abideenbooks@gmail.com

If you are interested to know more about **Yayasan Pendidikan Khalifah**, please visit

www.khalifahfoundation.com

If you are interested to explore more books published by **Abideen Books**, please visit abideenbooks.onpay.my

www.ingramcontent.com/pod-product-compliance
Lightning Source LLC
Chambersburg PA
CBHW031653040426
42453CB00006B/291